LITTLE PIECES OF LIGHT

Darkness and Personal Growth

Revised and Expanded Edition

JOYCE RUPP, OSM

Paulist Press
New York / Mahwah, NJ

Cover image by Phil McDonald / Shutterstock.com
Cover design by Sharyn Banks
Book design by Lynn Else

Library of Congress Cataloging-in-Publication Data
Names: Rupp, Joyce, author.
Title: Little pieces of light : darkness and personal growth / Joyce Rupp.
Description: Revised and Expanded Edition. | New York : Paulist Press, 2016. | Includes bibliographical references.
Identifiers: LCCN 2016001436 (print) | LCCN 2016008298 (ebook) | ISBN 9780809149834 (pbk. : alk. paper) | ISBN 9781587686047 (Ebook)
Subjects: LCSH: Suffering—Religious aspects—Christianity. | Consolation.
Classification: LCC BV4909 .R87 2016 (print) | LCC BV4909 (ebook) | DDC 248.8/6—dc23
LC record available at http://lccn.loc.gov/2016001436

ISBN 978-0-8091-4983-4 (paperback)
ISBN 978-1-58768-604-7 (e-book)

Published by Paulist Press
997 Macarthur Boulevard
Mahwah, New Jersey 07430

www.paulistpress.com

Printed and bound in the
United States of America

To:
my maternal grandmother,
Cecelia Meyer Wilberding,
who died in her forty-fourth year
giving birth to her thirteenth child

Contents

Music in the Dawn

Out of the shadowy, lingering abyss
wispy hints of the approaching dawn
gather mutely before the coming brilliance.
Songs of creation's glory stir in warm nests,
giving voice to the ancient joy residing
where darkness has yet to give way.

Robins warble melodies of hope
full of possibility and instinctual trust,
confident sunlight will follow
a steady course beyond the long silence
of past, opaque hours.

Their clear-throated, unbroken songs
resound with declarations of freedom,
encouraging strong wings to set forth
for bushes, meadow, forest, and stream.

Melodies continue to lift from the darkened nests,
a clear timbre unburdened by the complexities
humans construct in mind and heart.

These songs before the sun rises
call me to step away from the futile attempt
to control life.

They urge a release of my doubt,
put an end to my disbelief of ever shedding
this desolation.

Their hope-filled voices open up a truth
that something lies beyond
this night-drenched sorrow, this seemingly endless
interior darkness.

~Joyce Rupp

Acknowledgments

Each time I write a book, I am keenly aware of how I never do this by myself. It is both humbling and rewarding to remember how I have been influenced and guided by others' life experiences, expertise, and kindness. I'm particularly grateful to my colleagues who shared their editing skills and their perspectives on ministry to those in darkness: hospital chaplain Carola Broderick, marriage and family therapist Nicola Hiatt Mendenhall, and pastor Thomas Pfeffer. I thank Betty Pomeroy from New York for her invitation to speak to the Eastern regional gathering of hospital chaplains. The seeds for this book took root in my preparation for that conference. My Boulder Hospice interfaith dialogue group, David Chernikoff, Lynn Bijili Marlow, Nora Smith, and Diane Spearly have given me constant support and insights. The gracious Benedictine women of St. Walburga's Abbey in Boulder, Colorado, have allowed me space and solitude in their guest house where I have studied and written. Robert Wicks of Loyola College in Maryland invited me to write this book—his encouragement has been greatly appreciated. My editor, Maria Maggi, has been a delightful source of support for me. Then, there are those many "little pieces of light in my life," all the people who have offered love, prayer, and support to me—they are too numerous to mention all by name but they know that I know...and that I am deeply grateful. I especially thank my mother, Hilda Rupp, and Dorothy Sullivan, two women whose inner radiance has blessed my life.

Revised and Expanded Edition

In the midst of their full lives, the following generous souls paused to send their descriptions and lived experiences of "darkness," all of which you will find scattered throughout the pages of this book: Kathy Agamedi, Christine Bianco, Katie Bloom, Cindy Brown, Jean Clayton, Shirley Clement, Karin Ellis, Joan Freda, Julie Gardner, Mary Herlihy, Jan Hummel, Judith Kennedy, Patti King, Maureen Kolis, Mary Nordkvelle, Joyce O'Shea, Bobbie Paxton, Kathryn Pigg, Sabra Sandy, Sr. Ascenza Tizzano, Melissa Tuley, and Sue Whalen. Kathy Reardon graciously gave her ongoing support and keen eye to perusing my revisions. My fullest gratitude goes to Paul McMahon at Paulist Press. His editorial skills and personal kindness are some of the finest gifts an author could have.

God will enter into your night,
as the ray of the sun enters
into the dark, hard earth,
driving right down
to the roots of the tree,
and there, unseen, unknown,
unfelt in the darkness,
filling the tree with life,
a sap of fire
will suddenly break out,
high above that darkness,
into living leaf and flame.

~Caryll Houselander

Preface

"Are we going to listen to that darkness lady again?" I chuckled when a young mother mentioned this question her kindergarten-aged son asked her after she listened for several days to my talk on darkness and light while she took him to school. This incident occurred at least ten years ago. Now that her son has grown older, I wonder if what he heard back then influences his approach to the more difficult turns that come about as one grows into adulthood.

There certainly is no getting away from the reality that life does not always unfold as we wish. All sorts of disappointments, obstacles, painful incongruities, unfair circumstances, and harsh events hit us with force. Illness, accidents, termination of relationships, depression, financial dilemmas, deaths—and sorrows of all sorts we did not expect and certainly did not desire—come charging in with such fierceness they knock us off our inner and outer moorings. When this happens, light-filled happiness buries itself in a murky landscape inside of us. We find ourselves exiled from the person we thought we were and splintered apart from what gave us security.

When I began revising this book, I reached out to those receiving my monthly e-newsletter and invited them to send "a word, phrase, or one sentence" to describe their experience of this mutual lived reality. In doing so, I relearned how the experience of inner darkness touches most lives. As the e-mails poured in, I detected a certain kinship among those who contributed. Each definitely knew how it felt to be in the clutches of darkness. Their responses confirmed how this painful, unwanted visitor pushes its way in from time to time. The several hundred comments that arrived contained recurring, apt descriptions: "hopelessness, fear, dark hole, disconnection and isolation, deep longing, powerlessness, absence of joy, loss, alienation, separation from or abandonment by God."

Other depictions presented the situation more graphically and left little doubt as to the severe discomfort of this lightless occurrence: "drowning; captured inside a cocoon; heavy feeling of imprisonment; can't climb out of the pit; shrinking to nothing; slogging through a big, wet sponge; suffocating." Some people sent specific instances, such as "struggling to keep my home, divorce, death of a loved one, constant physical pain, the unexpected death of another son, a night spent in the emergency room with spinning vertigo and unrelenting nausea, my husband filled with self-doubt, the total indifference of my son."

A handful of responses verified a quite different view. These acknowledged the enriching qualities of darkness: "a blanket in wait, a pause for restoration, incubation and truth, necessary nightfall, a sleepover with God, holy solitude, loving presence, safe and warm within the womb of Earth before facing the bright light of day, a place where new life begins, the womb of creativity, awaiting the light of what is to be revealed, nurture, stillness, a loving embrace."

These descriptions confirmed another belief of mine regarding darkness: our lives would be incomplete without its life-sustaining facets. Macrina Wiederkehr and I emphasized these features eleven years after the publication of *Little Pieces of Light* when we collaborated in writing *The Circle of Life: The Heart's Journey through the Seasons.* As we composed our reflections and rituals, we felt it absolutely essential to accentuate the positive dimensions: the fetus growing in the mother's womb, the comfort of shade on a sweltering day, nighttime's restorative sleep, seeds germinating in black soil, glowing stars seen only in a darkened sky. We also wanted to assure persons of color that, rather than depreciating their life, their dark skin enhances it.

Music in the Dawn

Over twenty years have passed since I wrote *Little Pieces of Light.* As I look back, I find an ever-growing assurance regarding its basic message: the unwelcome parts of life hold the possibility of being catalysts for spiritual transformation. These undesired visitors often reveal more of who we truly are and gift us with greater awareness of what prevents us from being free to live as our most beloved selves. As we gradually move through the painful parts of darkness and find restored peace of mind and heart, we learn anew how to lean on the Compassionate One, whose tender embrace sustains and strengthens us, even when we do not sense this presence.

Although it may feel impossible at the time, we hold the potential to eventually grow through and beyond what shatters our inner harmony. Much depends on how we respond—on whether we stay open, in spite of our doubts, hesitations, and hopelessness. If we maintain trust that we will be shown little pieces of light along the way, we will have enough vision to sustain our strength while we endure the blurry dimness of the current situation.

One such piece of light came at a time when I was most in need of even the tiniest glimmer. It took place eleven years ago at 4:30 a.m. when I left Des Moines Mercy hospital after one of my most treasured friends died. My heart felt emptied of the likelihood of joy ever returning. My inner self dragged along as lifelessly as my body. Bereft and exhausted, I slogged along in the parking lot and headed toward my car. A few steps away from it, a sound I never heard before broke through the wall of deadness within me. Everywhere symphonic bird songs filled the air. Their melodies resonated through the entire city, or so it seemed. The beauty and breadth of their warbling wrapped around my sorrow and filled me with a kind of primal awe. I stopped walking. Listened. Became fully present to the incredible chorus. I couldn't believe what I was hearing. Then I perceived something more, these comforting, clear words: "They're singing his resurrection."

I knew then I could carry my desolation and find a way out of it. The heavy layer of bleak desolation plastered on my mind and heart would eventually ease and dissipate. There would come a time when joy returned. Hearing the birds singing their way out of night assured me not only of my friend's coming home to freedom and peace, but of my own ability to come out of the inner night, as well.

Not long ago on my daily walk, I entered the pre-dawn and without intending it to be so, I heard again a chorus of robins filling the air with their cheerful songs. Newly amazed, I instantly recalled my friend's death. I marveled at how free I now am of the inner gloom I felt back then. Gratitude rose and enveloped me as I returned in memory to the piece of light those feathered, early risers brought into my sorrow.

Introduction

One evening, a group of us gathered for a Pipe Ceremony to ritualize and bring to a close our course on Native American spirituality. Our leader, a Yaqui Indian who had lived on a Lakota reservation, invited us to help prepare the classroom for the ceremony. He explained that the room with its four windows needed to be in total darkness. This space without light would symbolize the womb of Mother Earth from which we had all come. He told us that as we prayed during the Pipe Ceremony, the blackened space would be a reminder that we were brothers and sisters, united as one in the Great Womb of Earth.

We set about the task of taping heavy black plastic garbage bags over all the windows. We even taped over the door frame to make sure all light would be eliminated from our space. Not one tiny crack or opening was to be left uncovered so the room could be as womblike as possible.

Finally, with everything tightly taped, we felt assured that when the lights were turned off, the darkness desired for the ceremony would be complete. We sat down in our circle as our leader stood by the door and pressed down the light switch. At first, an instant flood of blackness enveloped us. I felt as if I had fallen into a dark hole in space. Then, my eyes adjusted to the "hole" and I saw these tiny little pieces of light, the wee sunbeams of a strong summer sun that had not yet set. These little pieces of light penetrated infinitesimally small holes around the window frames that the taping had missed.

At that point, my life story stood up inside of me and took a quiet bow. "Yes," I thought, "this is what always sustains me in the tough times. No matter how thick the darkness, some unexpected light always shows itself. This reality convinces me I can live through dark experiences and not be completely overcome."

As I continued my ponderings during the Pipe Ceremony, I also recognized how I now approach darkness less as an enemy and more as a place of silent nurturance, where the slow, steady gestation needed for my soul's growth can occur. Not only is light a welcomed part of my life, I am also developing a greater understanding of how much I need to befriend my inner night times.

Darkness exists as a natural part of life, but I fought this reality for years. It always seemed like a powerful intruder into my light-filled life. I had this notion that if I thought or did the right things, then my life would always unfold the way I wished; I could avoid anguishing, bleak times. Consequently, when the dark moments showed up, I felt something must be terribly wrong with me. I presumed I had failed in some significant way because I had not figured out how to keep darkness from invading my life. It has taken a long time for me to acknowledge darkness as an essential element for personal growth. No matter how many "right things" I do, darkness will still come unannounced and uninvited because it is an essential part of personal growth and spiritual transformation. Without some darkness, I cannot become fully the person I am meant to be.

My acceptance of darkness as a help rather than a hindrance for growth developed through my personal experiences, by companioning others when they felt far from joy and peace, and through my studies. As I look back on my own painful episodes, I now see how much I learned from the very situations I wanted to toss out immediately. I also recognize how, in darkness, the light remains, perhaps totally hidden like the sun behind a heavy layer of clouds, but shining nonetheless.

I've read numerous books and articles that consider the descent into the unknown regions of ourselves as an indispensable part of spiritual and psychological growth. All agree we need light for our journey, but we also require darkness. Perhaps only those who have suffered and struggled can fully understand and accept the truth of this paradoxical process of transformation.

In *Little Pieces of Light: Darkness and Personal Growth*, I write about darkness from various perspectives with the anticipation that you, the reader, will gain courage and hope. May you find comfort and guidance, whether you are in your own valley of shadowed despondency or a companion to another who experiences it. May the little pieces of light that show up in your life penetrate the dark barriers and give you the power to sustain your courage as you continue onward.

CHAPTER ONE

The Land of Darkness

The land of darkness and shadow dark as death, where dimness and disorder hold sway, and light itself is like dead of night.

—Job 10:21–22

When I trained to be a hospice volunteer, an unexpected occurrence reminded me of how cutting and cruel darkness can be. One of the group exercises involved helping us learn how someone with a terminal illness might feel as increasingly more of what they cherish is taken from them. The facilitator gave each of us five small, square, white slips of paper. She asked us to think about what we most cherished in our lives and to write one of these on each of the five pieces of paper. Then she asked us to choose one of them and rip it up. I found this difficult to do. Next, she directed us to choose another labeled piece of paper and tear this one up, too. I found this action even more challenging. Then our facilitator said, "Please hold up your three remaining treasures with the words facing you." As we did so, she came to each of us, randomly picked out one of the papers, held it directly before our eyes, and very matter-of-factly tore it into pieces.

I'll never forget the moment she stood before me and took the one I considered the most valuable: "my spiritual life." Even though I knew her action was just a learning activity, my heart felt a stinging twinge of fear. At that moment, I not only understood on a gut level what a dying person might be going through, I also felt with my entire being the powerful letting go that a weighty darkness could demand of me.

Darkness comes in varied forms when "dimness and disorder" wipe out our strong hold on what we value. The *Merriam-Webster Dictionary* definition for the term *darkness* includes "closed, hidden, not easily understood, obscure, gloomy, hopeless, entirely or partly without light." This description hardly touches the human experience of getting lost in an extensive period of inner gloom.

Emotional, mental, and spiritual darkness develop due to any or all of the following:

> a time in which the energy and focus of life is almost completely funneled into physical, emotional, or psychic pain
>
> an experience of being buried in intense sorrow and grief
>
> a discouraging and empty inner sojourn when nothing seems valuable or worthwhile
>
> a stage of spiritual desolation in which there is no sense of a divine presence and little desire for things of the spirit
>
> a battle of indecision and struggle, when the

unknowns and fears of the future press
painfully upon decisions to be made

a fog-like state when life is confusing, unclear,
and seemingly impenetrable

a situation evolving from evil and atrocity that
threatens to overpower or annihilate

an excruciating time of helplessness in which
one feels paralyzed or powerless to alleviate
the pain of another

an ongoing siege of negativity that brings
with it constant frustration, irritation, and
dissatisfaction

a constant retraumatization due to painful
memories and disturbing nightmares

This list of general descriptions of darkness could go on and on. Some people move through these dim times recurrently, while others experience only occasional bouts when the "light itself is like dead of night." No one can say whose situation contains the greatest travail, but most experience some form of bleakness from time to time. Like Job, we long to have life return to the way it used to be or hope for it to be different in the future.

"Depression" is one of the most common labels given to inner darkness. Yet, even depression bears its own face in as many different ways as there are people. For some, this darkness exists as a lifelong valley of despair, often accompanied with thoughts of self-destruction. For others, depression brings a sporadic greyness that chills happiness and leaves the spirit blah. And yet, for others this darkness consists of foul moods with emotional responses such as anger, self-pity, guilt, sadness, bitterness, or apathy, pulling one down and hacking away at a positive attitude. Whatever form depression takes, it reflects a Job-like quality and most often coincides with the loss of self-esteem and deceptive mind-messages about who we are and the way life is.

Sometimes darkness develops when we face something unknown. It intrudes when we search for the missing pieces of truth about the past. Illness brings its own share of unknowns, too, especially when the illness persists without a diagnosis or becomes terminal. Questions about a shaky future may also contribute to one's darkness, as well as those disruptive life events that shatter our hopes and dreams or deprive us of anyone and/or anything we value and hold dear.

Darkness often breaks into our inner world when we experience the natural patterns of adult growth, such as midlife, retirement, and other significant aging processes. These natural developments challenge us to peer into our shadowy selves in order to accept traits we have not known, have refused to acknowledge, or have skillfully hidden from ourselves.

Life can go along well for quite some time and then, suddenly, we plop—kerplunk!—into the murky puddle. A member of a religious community in her eighties noted how she did not have any difficulty accepting the aging process until her eightieth birthday. Then, unexpectedly, she plunged into the depths of darkness in a way she had never known. This emotional nosedive called her to face her own mortality, and to admit the waning "light" of good health, easy energy, and physical mobility. This initial recognition left her feeling vulnerable, insecure, and helpless. Until this time, she had been able to brush aside the whispers of death and the question of what lies beyond this side of life.

Sometimes the land of darkness shows up as a spiritual wilderness, commonly referred to as "the dark night of the soul," a term used by the mystic John of the Cross. When the "dark night" arrives, the change can be quite terrifying because it seems we have lost the last link with hope: a relationship with the One who provides inner strength and vision. The voice of the soul cries out in utter abandonment, "Where do I go when the deepest Source of guidance and comfort apparently no longer abides with me?" The added torment of recognizing one's flaws and failures more clearly than ever often accompanies this sense of extreme loss.

Another form of darkness arises when discouragement and despair reach those who open their hearts to victims of atrocities and abuse. When anyone accompanies another's brutal suffering and severe pain with compassion, there's bound to be an effect on the mind and heart. The world's violence and destruction may draw a person into a mood of hopelessness or raw anger. The realization of collective evil can fall like a heavy, black cloud upon those who continually work for justice for the suffering ones of the world.

No matter what our lives involve, we rarely live without some dark moments pushing their way into our days. In spite of the distress they evoke, these periods of sparse light offer growth-filled opportunities. We require the darkness for our spiritual and psychological health, but this is a painful truth to accept. It's extremely difficult to believe this when we feel depressed. I've yet to hear anyone say, "Oh, I am so grateful. I woke up this morning feeling wretched and depressed. I know it's a good sign that I am in another stage of growth. I can't wait until this darkness intensifies some more."

Yet, darkness can be helpful and transforming if we are willing to stay open to it. Thomas Moore writes:

> The Greeks tell the story of the minotaur, the bull-headed flesh eating man who lived in the center of the labyrinth. He was a threatening beast, and yet his name was Asterion—Star. I often think of this paradox as I sit with someone with tears in her eyes, searching for some way to deal with a death, a divorce, or a depression. It is a beast, this thing that stirs in the core of her being, but it is also the star of her innermost nature.[1]

When the terrible flooding of 1993 occurred in the Midwest, a seventy-five-year-old woman described how she sat, watching the river rise around her home. She said, "It was the longest day of my life." During the flooding, her neighbors all joined together to protect her house with sandbags. They reached out to each other in ways they never had before. She described how one of them, whom everyone gossiped about as the local prostitute, offered the most concern and help during this treacherous time. This older woman never knew her neighbor well, but she welcomed the care and kindness of this supposed prostitute. The danger of Asterion in the flooding brought them together. The star of Asterion gave them a deeper respect for one another as loving humans who needed each other in a dark time.

We cannot completely avoid interior darkness. If we did so, we would be tossing out a vital part of our transformation.

Rather than getting rid of this robber of light, it profits us to search for ways to befriend it, as Joan Halifax indicates:

> We cannot eliminate the so-called negative forces of afflictive emotions. The only way to work with them is to encounter them directly, enter their world and transform them. They then become manifestations of wisdom. Our weaknesses become our strengths, the source of our compassion for others and the basis of our awakened nature.[2]

Does this mean we allow any and all kinds of abusive behavior, continue accepting addictive situations, wallow in meaningless depression, give in to an apathetic attitude of not caring what happens, or simply live with relationships that have gone sour and died? No, of course not. Yet, the fertilizer of our soul's growth lies in the midst of this darkness that we live with until we can change the situation.

We might know and believe intellectually that darkness serves as an essential conduit for our growth but still run from its presence emotionally. We only care about getting rid of the dreadful experience, moving on, and feeling good again. When darkness descends upon the human heart, we spend most of our energy doing battle with it rather than befriending it, thus missing the gift (the "star") it might be extending to us.

Any kind of darkness can call, push, nudge, and urge us onto the path of inner growth. It wakes us up and stirs questions in us we would rather not face:

How do the patterns of my thoughts and
behavior influence my life?

Whom or what have I hurt or taken for
granted?

Have I been attentive to the deepest longings of
my soul?

What asks to be "let go" in order for me to find
peace?

Who or what can help me make choices for the
future?

What do I really want to do with my life?

Whom do I want alongside me as I continue my
journey?

What am I really resisting or ignoring?

How is fear influencing my response to what is
happening?

Thought-provoking questions provide a clearer awareness about what wants to grow or change in us. They bring
new vision about "the way life is," helping us discover our
strengths and weaknesses with the consequent inner freedom to become who we truly are. The questions that darkness raises gift us with a willingness to live with insecurity
and allow us to find greater appreciation of the facets of life
we assumed would always be there for us.

In a sense, the darkness forces us inward. We can
attempt to sit the darkness out, or withdraw into ourselves,
or get completely absorbed in life's constant pressure of
activities. A much more healthy and growth-oriented option
consists of opening to the darkness, listening to what it has

to say, rather than simply enduring it or trying to boot it out the door as quickly as possible.

Even though we accept and befriend darkness as a part of the cycle of growth, we do not totally give in to it either. When we accept and befriend this visitor, it is like allowing someone to live in our house for a while but being emphatic and clear that this visit is temporary, not permanent. We cannot give the entirety of our time and concern to the darkness, even though this intrusive guest wants to take up all the space in our house.

We cannot simply withdraw and give the entirety of our resources to darkness. We must hold our own ground, stand up to it, and not let it push us around. If we allow darkness to take over our dwelling completely, it maims our inner world, rather than providing for our growth.

Living with this necessary balance takes constant effort. When we feel the tremendous power darkness exerts over us, we go to others, like ministers, therapists, spiritual directors, good friends, caring physicians, and wise persons, who are able to help us with the delicate balance of befriending darkness while also keeping a healthy distance from it. This balance is never easy to achieve, and with each visit of darkness, we learn the process all over again.

As we walk within the land of dim shadows, let us consistently hold two truths close to our hearts. First, darkness offers an opportunity for growth. Second, the time will come when night fades and light takes over again. We do not have to sit on the Job-like dung heap of darkness forever, but we must accept a place on it for a while.

Prayer

O God,
I have been to my inner place
where shadows dwell as dark as death.
I have been to the land of gloom
where my security shudders
and my dreams are coffined.
I want to believe and trust
that this land of desolation
contains a gift of growth for me.
Convince me. Assure me it is so.
Wrap this truth of transformation
firmly around my questioning heart.

~Joyce Rupp

Meditation

Find a quiet place where you can be alone for a while. Allow yourself to look into your life as you currently experience it. What do you see there? A wasteland devoid of life? A wide, swollen river threatening to overflow its banks? A vast, empty cave with desolate darkness? Something else? Picture yourself in that scene. Notice how your body, mind, and spirit respond. Then, imagine a Wise Guide coming to be with you. This Wise Guide approaches you with an understanding heart, knowing how life is for you now. Open your mind and heart to this compassionate presence.

Receive the guidance this Wise Guide has for you. Let it settle deep inside of you.

For Reflection/Journaling

1. After the meditation, record the guidance offered to you and your response to it. If you did not perceive or recognize any guidance offered, write about that experience. What would you have wanted to hear?

2. Turn to the list of questions in the chapter on page 12. Choose one that most calls to you and write your response.

3. How might you approach what you want to get rid of in your life so that a ray of hope can enter in?

CHAPTER TWO

Leave the Hall Light On

Too many of us panic in the dark. We don't understand that it's a holy dark and that the idea is to surrender to it and journey through to real light.[3]

—Sue Monk Kidd

Fear circled through the conversation between a small boy and his father in a television commercial urging parents to vaccinate their children as a prevention for childhood diseases. The television screen was completely black as the young boy, obviously in bed, called out to his father, "Dad, would you check the closet again? Are you sure there's no one under the bed?" The father kept reassuring him that nothing and no one was there. Finally, the two voices said good night to each other. A pause followed and then the tiny voice pleaded, "Dad, could you leave the hall light on?" Immediately following this typical evening conversation between a parent and child, an adult voice spoke from the distance, "There are some things you *should* be afraid of," with a message on the TV screen about where to seek vaccinations for children.

My heart leaned into this conversation for several reasons. I remembered my own childhood fear of the dark and how those imaginary sounds and shapes seemed like real persons and monsters. I also thought of how fear of the dark is not limited to childhood. It just changes direction as we move into adulthood. Instead of being afraid of the darkness *outside* of us, we focus our fear as adults on the darkness *inside* of us.

The voice saying there are some things we definitely ought to fear also resonated with me. We do need a healthy concern regarding dangerous darkness in order to be protected from what seeks to maim, wound, or destroy us. This kind of darkness consumes people's minds and sucks out their peace. Mentally ill patients whose battle never ends understand this, as do highly resentful, bitter persons who refuse to be healed. Dangerous darkness also lurks in situations where abuse, torture, or the destruction of another's life takes place. Wherever there is intimidation or a brutal taking away of life in any form, dangerous darkness resides.

Much of what we fear, however, occurs not so much as a threatening darkness but as a "holy dark," the kind we do not want but which provides opportunities for growth. This darkness stands in the way of our comfort, convenience, familiarity, security, desire for control, and "having it all together." This "holy dark" consists of situations that bring gloom, struggle, and depression. They feel like a curse but actually contain a blessing. These "holy dark" occurrences bear the touch of God's grace and wait to transform us if only we allow it.

When we yearn for life to return to how we once knew it or to change for the better, we tend to feel as though a part of our self has disappeared. Not surprisingly, this sense of loss brings about emotions associated with grief. Anger surfaces as a rage against the dark. We feel overwhelmed, get on our pity-pots, withdraw, or hide out in an effort to avoid these emotional responses. We may feel confused, irritable, or restless, or perpetuate a constant state of busyness in an effort to escape the unending grim days and nights.

External events also evoke similar emotions. When we no longer have a person, creature, profession, or anything claiming our heart, a part of our self feels like it died. And maybe it has. Maybe this part has to die, or get out of the way, or be lost for a while so that another part of us can be uncovered or given due attention. We long to retrieve this lost part of us hidden in the gloom or dying on the roadside of our pain. At the same time, another part of us waits to be discovered, crying out, "Look at me! Listen to me! I long to be embraced by you!" but we refuse to hear what it has to say because we are absorbed in the emotions accompanying our darkness.

A woman at a retreat related the story of her deep and long journey of darkness. It began when she was forced to retire from a teaching position at a university because of her age. She described how unfair this decision felt because she still had a lot of energy and vitality. Depression, anger, and alienation wrapped themselves around her heart. Fear took over and she felt certain she would have nothing more to offer others; that her gifts and enthusiasm would turn to ashes. She allowed this fear to dominate her moods and behavior, and she withdrew from people and activities.

After being in this hostile, dark world for over two years, the pastor of her local parish invited her to a meeting in which he spoke about the great need for visitors to care for the older, disabled, shut-in members of the parish. Fearful and hesitant, she moved into this work. To her amazement, she enjoyed the new challenge, and as she told me, "I love this work more than anything I've ever done in my life." Only when this woman "lost" the teaching part of herself did the pastoral, hospitable part rise up and make itself known.

Fear shoves through our security, our intelligence, and all the wisdoms we've learned. This emotion wheedles its way into our mind and convinces us of all sorts of untruths. Fear manages to misdirect our path and lead us astray with its spooky voice and false suggestions. As Bryce Courtenay writes, "The imagination is always the best torturer."[4] Fear of the unknown or of the consequences of the darkness plays a major role in our imagination. It torments us with questions and shows us illusory monsters of the future.

Doubts and haunting interrogations rise up and threaten to choke our hope: "Will this ever end? Am I doing the right thing? Will I find my way out of this maze? How can I live without this person? Can I open myself to love again? Will I be able to adapt to my changed body?" When I allow fear to take over my imagination, I often believe the darkness will overpower me and I will not be able to find my balance. I fear being beaten down forever, that I will always feel lonely, desolate, and empty and will never regain my energy or my taste for joy and beauty.

Carol Pregent described her wrestling with darkness and the fear of never having her life together again in this way:

> I feel fragmented, broken in pieces like a puzzle
> all spread out on the table. None of the pieces

are together and I am not even sure if they will fit together. There are so many pieces that I fear I will not be able to put them back together. Is it an insurmountable task?[5]

Sometimes dread rises up in us and actually brings on the darkness. Anxiety tends to surface when enormous risks come or when a significant departure approaches, such as a child soon to leave home for adult life. Apprehension may loom large when the wide gap in a relationship becomes increasingly apparent or when aging parents become noticeably frail and fragile. A quiet trepidation may be present when some haunting and unwanted truth begins to signal from the depths of our beings.

What can we do about our fear when light hides from us? Accept it as a natural response to darkness. Expect fear to arrive and acknowledge its presence. Stephen Levine tells the story of how an old man, a great Tibetan saint, was meditating one day when three dark figures came to his cave. They were "rattling skulls and bloody swords, shrieking obscenities and exuding the smell of rotten flesh." The great saint looked up, gave them a smile and invited them to "take tea." The dark figures expressed amazement at his lack of terror. The old man replied that he was grateful to be on the path of healing and that their ugliness only reminded him "to be aware and have mercy."[6]

Most fears never actually happen. They try to keep us in our place by acting like bullying Goliaths pushing around the little David in each of us, seeking to paralyze us with inaction so we do not develop greater freedom and wholeness. A good friend cured me of much of my anxiety by always asking in my dark times, "What's the worst possible thing that could happen?" Then, "How probable is this?" Those questions provided a good reality check and helped to put some distance between my fear and what was actually happening. By taking a close look at what is real and what is from the imagination, we can lessen the power fear has over us.

We need to face what frightens us in dark times. These anxieties extract a lot of energy from us when we ignore or deny them. They can dominate our lives and leave us continually stress-filled. In Ursula LeGuin's Earthsea trilogy, a dark thing kept chasing the main character, Ged, who felt increasing terror. Ged ran and ran and ran from this dark shadow of a thing. The faster he ran from this eerie form, the faster it ran after him. Finally, Ged could run no more. Exhausted and exasperated, in a whirl of desperation, he turned around and faced the huge dark thing. At that precise moment, when Ged confronted this looming figure, the dark thing turned around and ran for its life.

A true story of a brutally raped woman reveals a similar response to fear. Even after he was convicted of the crime, she continued to be psychologically traumatized by her rapist. She lived with constant panic and suspicion. Finally, when this anguished woman reached near her breaking point, she made a decision to visit her rapist at the county jail. There she confronted him with her anger and demanded an apology. He never gave her one, but choosing to see him face-to-face gave her back her power, and she broke the stronghold that the darkness of the rape had on her.[7]

Our worst fears must be faced: "What is it that scares me so much?" We call on our Loving Source of Power to help us turn around and look at it, whether that fear is named loneliness, vulnerability, illness, failure, dying, joblessness, lack of identity, rejection, loss of faith, or any other thing terrorizing our hearts and minds. I've learned that when I turn around and look at my fear, it never carries the immense power it first had over me. I might shudder and shake when I meet it, but I also know it does not have to conquer me unless I allow it to do so. The more I believe in the possibility of darkness to activate my personal growth, the less power fear will have over me.

Besides facing my fear, I must also learn how to discipline my mind so I dwell on other things. I cannot ignore what I imagine, but I also cannot allow it to hang around and torment me all day. I can "have tea" with my fear for a certain amount of time, but then I send it on its way. Talking about my imagined concerns with a safe person or group also lessens their grip. As I speak my fear out loud, it gets weaker and I become stronger. I find comfort, too, in knowing others understand my fears and may well have had similar ones. Finally, I also need to "lighten up" when I am in darkness. How easy it is to toss aside my sense of humor when life is bleak. Yet, this is when I most need to activate it.

It does become easier to live in the darkness the more we see this phase of our lives as just that, a phase—a necessary part of our humanity—that we trust will eventually pass. A colleague once asked if the pain and turmoil he experienced would ever cease. Much later in life, when he had moved through this stage, he told me, "The one thing I kept clinging to and that gave me hope was when you answered my question, 'Does it get better?' with 'Yes, it does. It may take a while, but it does get better.'"

This darkness *will* lessen. I must believe this. But I must also accept that I will never be exactly the same as before I experienced it. This harsh intruder will affect my life. When I am in the midst of it, I can hardly envision anything except a negative change, but surprisingly, positive developments will unfold if I choose to stay open to the process.

As I face my fear, I do need a "hall light on"—an assurance of a way out of the mess eventually, knowing someone is there to offer kindness and support as I wait in the dense obscurity. Sometimes my "hall light" has consisted of another person who never gave up on me. Other times my only "hall light" has been faith in the divine presence. When darkness was extremely private or unnamed, I could only find solace in the One I knew would never let me go. I have often taken comfort in Psalm 23: "Even though I walk through the darkest valley, I fear no evil; for you are with me."[8]

Stories from scripture assure me of this divine solace because the Holy One continually gives two messages over and over to the women and men who go through challenging times: "Do not fear" and "I am with you." I find great comfort in these assurances and clutch them to my empty heart when times are tough.

Prayer

O God,
I am afraid in the darkness.

I pull the sheets of security around me
and view my imaginings with terror.
These fears rise up in the shadows of my soul,
like wild warriors ready to attack me.
Though I hide from these monsters of my making,
or attempt to flee on the road of anxiety,
they are always pursuing, close behind me.
Help me to turn around and face my fears.
Do not let them have power over me.
May I not succumb to the terrors of my mind
that chase me relentlessly in the darkness.

~Joyce Rupp

Meditation

Sit or lie down. Become aware of the power of your breath sustaining your life. With each in-breath, say the word "peace." Do this until stillness settles in you. Then visualize yourself in a small room with almost no light. Notice what it is like for you emotionally and mentally as you sit in this darkness. After you do so, imagine an angel of love coming to be with you. Welcome this strengthening messenger as best you can. Allow the angel of love to comfort and console you. Notice how the darkness lessens in intensity when you open your mind and heart to this trusted presence. Lean on this love and absorb it into your deep self.

For Reflection/Journaling

1. Write a letter to the angel of love.
2. Describe any fears you might have. Then turn to each fear and express what you want to say to it about the thoughts and feelings it evokes in you.
3. Read Psalm 23. Recall any fears that are taking away your confidence and peace. Write your own psalm.

CHAPTER THREE

Silent Stirrings in the Tomb

But I shall be wise this time and wait in the dark...[9]

—Rabindranath Tagore

I like to envision myself outside the emptied Easter tomb, sitting there with the joyful angel or marveling with the surprised Mary as she hurries away to announce the good news of resurrection (John 20:1–2). But the thought of being inside that airless, eerie tomb with its damp smell of death does not entice me at all. My strong inclination toward light bids me to ignore Holy Saturday, the day of "in between." The part of me that resists waiting wants to hide from the unknown and the uncontrolled, while resurrection with its abundant, vibrant life attracts me. I'd much rather forget the Easter tomb was once occupied or that the tiny green bud on the bush once found itself encased in ice and snow. In the same way, I tend to forget that the wisdoms guiding my life once lay dormant in the dim corridors of myself.

I wonder if it might be this way for most people. I have certainly found this to be the case with my own Christian faith. Most pastors and parishioners ignore Holy Saturday, the "day of in between," with rituals focused on Good Friday and the celebration of Easter. Whatever happened to the significant, symbolic event of time in the tomb? This absolutely essential part of the story tends to be ignored, set aside, or forgotten. Yet, Easter cannot happen without this waiting stage.

Resurrection occurs only after the tomb encloses a resident. Psychologist C. G. Jung indicates the tomb or cave as the place where "a person goes when there is a great work to be accomplished, an effort from which one recoils."[10] Renewal, whether of the earth or the human heart, contains its own "Holy Saturday" when the darkness smells of death and shows no evidence of movement. Yet, unseen during this period, life stirs, moves, and changes into something surprising.

I do not intend to sound poetic or idealistic when writing about the tomb as a gestation time. There's nothing "romantic" about interior darkness. Just ask anyone who is languishing in memories of a loved one who's died, or who is excruciatingly ill, or despairing to the point of contemplating suicide, or desperately clutching at the last bits of self-worth. These people do not experience darkness as some charming companion who comes along and says, "I have a new revelation for you."

This place of "in between" contains agonizing silence and painful hollowness. Throughout the ages, various sages and writers have attempted to describe it: tomb, underworld, womb, cave, desert, chrysalis, and so on. The metaphors all bear the same mark: a dark, waiting space of transformation.

William Bridges uses the term "neutral zone" to characterize this seemingly unproductive stage of growth:

> We aren't sure what is happening to us or when it will be over. We don't know whether we are going crazy or becoming enlightened....For many people the experience of the neutral zone is essentially one of emptiness in which the old reality looks transparent and nothing feels solid anymore."[11]

I thought about this while walking one Holy Saturday on a hiking path I had discovered in the foothills of the Rockies. The trail meandered through a canyon, along a narrow, recently melted, lively creek. The fresh green of the earth left little doubt of spring's arrival. Tiny, ripe buds of bushes and grasses particularly caught my eye. I had never looked so closely at buds to see what a variety of hues they possessed: magenta, lime green, brown, orange, tan, red, and deep purple. They seemed to call with some significant message, so I stood there for a long while and waited for what I might hear.

As I lingered, I marveled at the power of life pushing the buds toward openness. I thought of how they patiently waited, waited, waited for the right moment before they could rise from their wintered tombs. Then I heard the message they offered: In the neutral zone, the winter season of the heart when all seems dead and barren, the potential for life is being nurtured and readied for the hurrah of springtime. In the winter, who would believe the empty branches of those bushes would ever sing with sweet green again? In the tomb times of our lives, who of us would ever believe that our hearts would be singing again with the sweet sounds of joy and eagerness?

There's a power in the plant that fills the bud and responds to the warmth of sunlight and to the moisture pushing up from the roots, much like the power of the Eastered tomb when the linens fell off and the Risen One emerged into the golden glow of morning. Similarly, the power of the Radiant Light in us urges us to stay in the struggle, to wait in the dark, to believe in the value of this stage of our journey, and to trust that our own budding and blossoming will come again.

Having to wait and wait and wait without answers, without direction or an easing of the emptiness, frequently results in excruciating anxiety. Eastering cannot be rushed or forced. There are no clocks or calendars telling us when our inner resurrection will happen. No baby in the womb has ever seen a map that said "this way out." The child has to wait until the push of the contractions thrusts the womb door open. No seed in the soil has a sign pointing "this way up." No, the seed waits until the warmth penetrates the soil and draws the first sheath of green from beyond the opened shell. No butterfly developing in the chrysalis has a schedule and a timetable posted next to her. No, she waits and gives herself to the unfolding process. Jesus, too, had to wait until the angels came and unbound him from the burial shroud. ("They took him down from the tree and buried him in a tomb. But *God raised him* from the dead" [Acts 13:29–30].)

Maureen Murdock refers to this struggle in her tomb-like description of the symbolic descent to the underworld:

In the underworld there is no sense of time; time is endless and you cannot rush your stay…. This all-pervasive blackness is moist, cold, and bone-chilling. There are no easy answers in the underworld; there is no quick way out. Silence pervades when the wailing ceases. One is naked and walks on the bones of the dead.[12]

When we plant a seed in the soil or a caterpillar spins a cocoon, there's no way of telling what's going on inside or exactly how long the stay is going to be. We cannot dig up the seed to check if there's growth or slip open the cocoon and peek inside, because each of these actions would cause death. We can't peer into the tomb of ourself and see if something grows in there either. It's truly a journey of trust in the transformative process. All kinds of inner stirrings go on, but we simply cannot detect them taking place. We trust the growth necessary for our life's journey will develop, without being able to know this is happening.

Once when speaking with a group, I recall using the example of a little creature in a chrysalis that silently hangs while all sorts of phenomenal changes take place. I asked, "Who would ever believe a monarch butterfly would come forth from that dark, brown sack?" One of the participants quickly spoke up, "Yeah, well it's easy for that creature. But for me, when I'm in my dark time, I can't just hang there and wait to be born. I have to shower, grocery shop, care for my children, get to work, and more." She was right, but the reality remains: we cannot hurry the "in between" time, and we cannot know in the womb of our darkness what our growth will look like until we eventually resurrect.

A number of resources and therapeutic curatives subtly claim "if you read this, do this, experience this...then the darkness will quickly vanish." This approach implies that "if you think the right things, give yourself the correct messages, find the best teacher, and so on," you won't have any darkness in your life. This false voice actually detains or stalls our journey of growth because transformation rarely occurs with only light as its source.

Meaningful or inspiring resources such as an insight from someone, a positive mental image, an affirming message, or a suggested spiritual practice do have the potential to sustain us or point us toward our growth, but we still have to contend with the waiting period. Caring therapists, ongoing support groups, deep meditation, healing music, or energizing workshops can assist in guiding, consoling, comforting, or freeing us as we go through the bleakness, but they won't make the waiting disappear. When darkness seems to "instantly vanish," or to never be a part of our lives, it is usually being repressed or denied and will make a return appearance at a later unnamed time and place. We can do all the "right things," but sooner or later, we have to live for a while in that tomb-like experience of waiting, wondering if the light will ever reappear.

How readily nature accepts this dark passageway of life—snakes shed their skin, birch trees say goodbye to their bark, lobsters leave their shells behind at least seven times, caterpillars spin their own dark homes, and polar bears crawl into their caves of hibernation for a lengthy season of inactivity. But we humans scream out against this "leaving behind" and "letting go." Sitting in the darkness and waiting doesn't come naturally for us even though each of us "sat" for nine months in our mother's womb, a development as mysterious and marvelous as that of a caterpillar metamorphosing into a butterfly.

The Hebrew Scriptures tell the story of the people who hurried out of Egypt's slavery and traveled for years and years in an unknown wilderness. These people thought they were just wandering around directionless, lost, and abandoned, with few positive things happening while they wended their way to the "promised land." As they did so, however, they learned much about their faith, their insecurities, their strengths and weaknesses. During this long sojourn, the people of the Exodus story discovered the immense power of the Holy One's faithful love and the resilience of their own spirits. Only when they came to the promised land of Canaan and looked back at their wanderings did they truly understand the transforming effects of their desert experience.

Jesus recognized the necessity of going through the "in between" stage long before he went through it in his own passion and death. He urged his followers to be willing to let go, or to die to self, in order to be more fully alive. But messages like "lose your life to find it" and "the grain of wheat has to fall into the ground and die or it stays just a grain of wheat" often become lost in our fear of having to spend time in the dark waiting room of uncertainty and not knowing (cf. Luke 9:24; John 12:24). Still, the reality remains: certain parts of who we think we are will need to change radically if we are going to grow. This changing happens in those dark times of the unknown when we have little to which we can cling and a lot to surrender. The cross has to be carried; the old self has to be shed. This journey requires a tremendous amount of letting go and "dying" to what gives comfort and security. Thus, it brings with it some inherent anxiety.

In the former communion rite of the Roman Catholic Eucharist, the celebrant prayed that the Lord "keep us free from sin and protect us from all anxiety." I used to think this plea a rather ridiculous, impossible concept. As I have grown in understanding the necessity for darkness as a part of the journey of growth, I now recognize the wisdom of this prayer. While it may seem unlikely for the human heart to be protected from all anxiety, peace becomes possible when we accept the value of waiting in the womb of growth. The more I am convinced of this, the less I need to fret and worry as I usually do when dark times arrive. Trust in the process of interior growth requires a giant leap and takes a lifetime of effort. I must be patient with myself and with the process.

Some people learn this lesson of transformation well. I heard someone who had seen more than his share of life's adversities remark, "Well, what do you expect? You can't do a long jump and not expect to get some sand in your shorts." After I stopped laughing, I remember thinking to myself how much I wanted to have more of that attitude. I expect life to be neat, clean, and tidy, not messy, disruptive, confusing, and irritating. I don't like "sand in my pants." But this is not the way of transformation. Whether the darkness comes from external events or from some inner call bidding me to go deeper, it leads to much greater personal freedom to be my best self when I expect and accept the "sand."

We always try to have a balance—to enter freely into the waiting room of darkness and yet not gorge ourselves on the pain and discomfort. We have probably met people who wear their woes and old hurts like a breastplate of self-importance. It's their way of drawing attention to themselves, of deriving some long-sought human care and compassion, or of meeting some other deep need.

The stirrings in the tomb of darkness are the whispers of our soul, urging us to move toward a place we have not been before. We may be pushed to make changes we would otherwise never have considered. We may be forced to look at hidden wounds and inner issues we were always able to shove aside. We may be led to appreciate life and our gifts at a more extensive and deeper level. Usually the womb of darkness provides a catalyst for creativity and a fuller relationship with the Holy One. Always it is a time for trust in the transformative process and for faith that something worthwhile may be gained by our waiting in the dark.

Prayer

O God,
I wait in the unending darkness
like a chrysalis on a lonely limb.
I am living in the dreadful "in between"
of death and life, of darkness and light,
not coming, not going, just hanging on.
I fight the seeming emptiness
and struggle against required surrender.
Teach me to wait patiently,
while my wings grow strong,
for my time of flying has not yet come.

~Joyce Rupp

Meditation

Imagine being in a darkened tomb. You can smell the musty odor of the damp stone. You are not alone. A kind and caring Presence is with you, wrapped around your being like a gentle, protective veil. Sit in this dark space and listen to your deep self. Allow the Veil of Protection to absorb what is most difficult for you. Sense your body, mind, and spirit being cleared of what keeps peace from being present. When you are ready, let yourself move out of the tomb. Breathe clean air. Stretch your limbs with life-giving energy. Turn your heart toward the Veil of Protection that remains with you. Open yourself as fully as possible to receive what this beloved Presence offers.

For Reflection/Journaling

1. Draw a tomb. Inside the tomb, sketch symbols or write words to describe your experience of being in the tomb space.
2. Write the word "in-between" at the top of the page. Beneath this word, list specifics that might help you to be patient with this dark waiting room of your inner world (such as resources, persons, aspects of nature, scripture, social connections, art, and so on).
3. What do you find most challenging about waiting? What or who would you want to assist you in being able to wait more peacefully?

CHAPTER FOUR

Separate Bedrooms

I know what it feels like to want God like I want my own breath. I know what it feels like to experience nothing but darkness and silence.[13]

—Macrina Wiederkehr

We sat in a circle as we opened the retreat on transitions. I asked the group to share their names and one thing they wanted the group to know about themselves. When it came time for a petite, thirty-five-year-old woman to speak, she gave her name and said, "If I were to describe my relationship with God, I'd say it was like separate bedrooms."

Her unexpected, surprising remark met with laughter but was followed by a compassionate, somber silence as she went on to describe her anger and despair after recently learning her cancer had reoccurred for the third time. She emphasized her distress by saying, "I'm angry as hell at God" and noted that coming to the retreat was the last thing she should probably be doing. "In fact," she said, "I may not even stay for this whole thing."

What this despondent woman experienced is not unusual. Our life with the Holy One is bound to be affected when the other parts of our life exist in a wasteland. We cannot isolate our spiritual life and "freeze it" in a perpetual state of happiness while the rest of our self mourns and thrashes in the valley of darkness.

As a spiritual director who has traveled dark journeys myself and also accompanied others in their disconsolate times, I find some common responses, or natural consequences, that affect our spirituality. Once in a while, a person in darkness continues to feel a strong bond with the Divine. This relationship is what gets that person through the desolate journey. But for most, this experience does not happen. Rather, a vast chasm of separation grows between us and the One who sustained us in the past. No matter how we try to pray or worship, this formerly intimate Presence seems hidden and unavailable.

Often when we try to pray in the foggy stage of transformation, our prayer tastes like sawdust. We have absolutely no felt experience of a divine presence. Our spiritual world feels empty and barren. We leave our time of prayer wondering if it was worth the effort. Oftentimes this emptiness leads to boredom and a "who cares" attitude, including a loss of desire for a spiritual practice. Our head says, "You ought to try to stay connected," but the rest of us fights doing so because the One who is supposed to be near appears unreachable.

During this estrangement, a strong restlessness interferes when we attempt to pray. We cannot concentrate or sit still. This produces even more thoughts and feelings of hopelessness and increases an excruciating response of feeling as though we have failed miserably.

Questions about the Holy One's nearness or presence abound. We may feel as though we've been abandoned by the Presence we thought would never leave us. We ask ourselves whatever happened to those glorious promises in the scriptures that assured us: "I will be with you." Anger or disappointment with God pushes its way through as we feel this abandonment.

We can find ourselves becoming highly impatient with the Holy One or with ourselves. We expect so much and so little is happening. Our mind keeps badgering us with edgy thoughts: "If I'm being faithful to my spiritual life, why don't I feel any better?" "How long will this go on?" "Will I ever feel the Holy One's nearness again?"

Along with impatience, guilt wheedles its way into our darkness. Little messages creep into our discomfort: "I should be able to pray," "Maybe if I just prayed longer," "I ought to feel better about this. I must be doing something wrong." We start to doubt our choice of prayer and look for other ways to pray, thinking this might change things.

Our perception of divinity generally faces challenges during a time of darkness. A comment such as "I don't know who to pray to anymore" expresses the frustration of being unable to name a formerly identified divinity. This confusion adds to a sense of distancing from this close Companion and makes it even tougher to stay connected.

When darkness evolves into despair or depression and thoughts of suicide surface, all hope of a divine being lifting the burden of darkness disappears. Prayer eventually becomes less a beating against the blank wall of separation and more a total and complete withdrawal from God into a hollow space of nothingness.

How challenging to believe this unyielding barricade could be a part of our personal growth. Yet, there are numerous ways in which the darkest moments of our spiritual lives teach us and guide us to new vision and deeper living. We must keep open in our darkness because we may well learn something about our relationship with the Holy One, as author Ann Keiffer confirms:

> I hauled my depression from sanctuary to sanctuary, but found no sanctuary. I was a spiritual misfit and went away all the more depressed that I could not embrace these churches or feel embraced by them. Maybe I'd come to a bad time, and God wasn't in right then. Actually, God was in. In the place I hadn't looked yet: in the depths of depression.[14]

Darkness sometimes invites us to reconsider our notion of God. What we believe about the Divine has an effect on our life, particularly when we are going through a difficult time. If we believe the Holy One got us into the mess, or if we think we've done something wrong and are being punished for it, or if we see divinity as some sort of "instant fixer of all ills," we will fall more deeply into the pit of darkness.

Our understanding and our metaphors for the divine being may be too limiting for our adult lives. Perhaps we are being stretched into considering the dark One of the womb, as well as the One of light. ("Even darkness to you is not dark, and night is as clear as the day" [Ps 139:12].) Maybe we need to move beyond the One who judges us to the One who loves us totally, without any reservations. We might be challenged to welcome the feminine qualities of divinity, as well as the masculine ones. As with anything we value and have to let go, it is not easy to welcome an aspect or belief about divinity that calls us beyond the way we currently relate or believe.

The darkness may also provide an opportunity to look more closely at our weaknesses, which we have heretofore avoided. Recognition of our less-than-perfect selves brings us greater clarity regarding our humble dependence on the grace of the Holy One to transform us. During an extended retreat, I first recognized my inner possibilities for evil. This became an overwhelming darkness for me when I named this part of myself. However, the truths I learned during this experience brought some of my greatest gifts. They helped me become a much more open, nonjudgmental listener to the faults and failings of others. These truths also enabled me to extend more compassion and understanding toward myself, now that I know I can't manage my struggle for goodness all by myself.

Whenever I go through an occurrence of darkness, I almost always feel called to let go of something and to accept being out of control in some way. I fight this but eventually see how I am not the sole manager of my spiritual journey. There are parts of me that need to be surrendered. My ego, or my "I," demands so much and keeps a tough hold on me, so I am not free to grow in ways necessary for my personal development. Sometimes it takes the vulnerable and defenseless posture of darkness to free my strong grasp on my ideas or my secure ways of praying.

In my twenties, I saw a foreign film titled *The World of Apu*. The only piece of this film I remember astounded me then and still does today. Apu had written reams of paper containing his philosophical concepts and experiences. At a certain point in his life, he went through a deep and long depression. At the end of this era of emptiness, Apu sat on a high hill with the stacks of paper in his lap. He very deliberately tossed every one of the papers to the wind, which carried them away from him forever. That profound gesture of total surrender gave Apu the freedom he needed to move on with his life.

In my youth, I thought it absolutely crazy to toss those papers to the wind. As an older adult, I still cringe at what Apu did, but I now see there is no other way except to "throw things to the wind" if I am to continue to grow. Surrender to the Holy One persists as an essential part of growth on the spiritual journey. Sometimes this growth demands relinquishment of what I hold most closely to my heart.

Being able to let go demands a tremendous amount of trust in our Faithful Companion. Thomas Merton writes that "true love and prayer are really learned in the hour when prayer becomes impossible and your heart turns to stone."[15] In the hour of our greatest darkness, when we eventually discover we are never truly alone, we realize divine love is much more than we ever imagined. We learn to trust that God sits there with us in our shadow of death even though we cannot touch this presence with our human longing.

> When we enter the spiritual night, we can feel alone, encompassed by a fearful darkness. What we need to remember is that we're carried in

God's womb, in God's divine heart, even when we don't know it, even when God seems far away.[16]

I finally accepted that the Holy One does not leave my vulnerable self when I went into the hospital for an operation. I had no idea how wretched and helpless I would feel when I came out of surgery. As the anesthetic gradually wore off and the pain increased, I looked over and recognized a member of my community sitting in the corner of the room. She extended such kindness by staying with me the entire day. I knew Camilla could not take the pain away, but I drew immense comfort from her being there with me. That is how I envision God being with us in our time of darkness. This loving presence sits in a corner of our darkened room of pain. We are not left alone while we struggle, learn, grow, and heal. We can count on this Compassionate One to be with us.

I find remarkable comfort in knowing the Holy One never leaves me. Many years ago, a psalmist who must have known firsthand the terrors of the darkness wrote this verse: "In the shadow of your wings I take refuge, until the destruction is past" (Ps 57:1). Taking shelter in the shadow of these wings won't take away the darkness, but it does ease the dread of its length and intensity.

The woman at the retreat who described her relationship with God as "separate bedrooms" did have a consoling moment during the retreat. This occurred on the day we listened to a song by Colleen Fulmer titled "Rock Me Gentle."[17] The refrain pictures us being comforted in the arms of God as tenderly as an infant is rocked in the arms of a loving parent. This woman came to me afterward with tears on her cheeks and whispered, "That's what I need—oh, yes—to just be held by God."

Knowing this truth of the Holy One's nearness does not keep us from the natural consequences of the spiritual journey. We may be rocked and cradled in the arms of compassion, but we still face the painful terms of transformation. I continue to want a cozy divine presence who lets me escape the difficult stages, rather than one who leaves me empty and refuses to rescue me from my darkness until more of my transformation occurs. In other words, there is simply no way to get out of the tough stuff, no matter how intimate, deep, and strong our relationship with God. There has to be a real "dying" internally in order to find new life.

What do we do, then, when we are experiencing the bleak land of darkness in our spiritual lives? Besides striving to accept the darkness as a part of our growth, we stay faithful. We keep crying out, bringing our tired, empty selves to this Sacred Source of Love. We let our feelings just be there and do not give up on the journey. The light never goes out for us; it only hides behind the clouds of our present situation. The Holy One is just as present with us in our dark times as in our well-lighted ones. We ought not to give up on this loving presence when we are most in need of this relationship.

Trying new forms of prayer can be helpful. In fact, this might be part of the new growth awaiting us. This entails trying a completely different way of relating to the Hidden One. I've known people who've walked or danced their way through dark times. Others have used clay or paints or comforting music to stay connected with the Inner Presence whom they cannot feel.

And yes, some cry their way through the dark times. Allowing tears and sorrow to fill our prayer is another way to bring all we are to the One who loves us tenderly and completely. The form of prayer really does not make any difference. The important thing is to make the effort to stay connected.

Sometimes we may gain courage in our present dryness by returning in memory to the past when we experienced emptiness and discouragement. We look back and see how we grew from a difficult time. How did that experience shape and affect who we are today? What was the wisdom gained? How are we different now?

Our relationship with God hungers to be nourished. The fire in us with barely a glint of flame yearns to be lit. The Divine Light is not limited to being present only in formal worship or personal prayer. This love permeates our whole being. Thus we tend to the various dimensions of who we are, even when we feel too weary or dismal to care about anything. This can be done in various ways: through reading inspiring books, listening to music that touches our souls, spending time with the earth or with caring persons, exercising our bodies, or going to an energizing sports game, an art gallery, or a film. Even when we drag ourselves halfheartedly to these activities, we silently proclaim a belief that the fire has not gone out and that we are still willing to tend it.

I appreciate the Hebrew Scriptures for their honesty about the darkness we humans experience. People are allowed to cry out their pain and woe to the Holy One. Rather than the darkness being denied, we are given the assurance that it will pass in time, and a happier phase of life will eventually unfold. Psalm 13:1–2, 5 is an example of this:

How long, Yahweh, will you forget me? For ever?
How long will you turn away your face from me?
How long must I nurse rebellion in my soul,
sorrow in my heart day and night?

As for me, I trust in your faithful love....
Let my heart delight in your saving help,
let me sing to Yahweh for [Yahweh's] generosity
    to me,
let me sing to the name of Yahweh.

We need to keep the spark of hope alive in us and cry out to the Holy One from the empty places of our hearts. What feels like "separate bedrooms" to us is only that: a feeling. In the deepest center of our souls the eternal presence of divinity resides, rocking us gently, urging us to believe in the value of the dark dimensions of our inner voyages.

Prayer

O God,
after all the time we've spent together,
I never thought it would come to this—
an immense chasm carved between us,
holding the empty echoes of my prayer.

Only a tiny voice remains
of my worn-out cries longing for you.

Where are you, God, when I need you most?
Why won't you fix my life for me?
I need you to get me out of this darkness.
I demand that you give me extended bliss.

But my demands and my desires go unheeded
and all I hear is a tender voice
whispering repeatedly, "I am with you."

~Joyce Rupp

Meditation

Find a place that holds as much silence as possible. Sit down in that place and receive the silence. There is no need to do anything. Just "be" with the stillness. Let any thoughts and feelings that arise float away. Give yourself to the wordless silence and welcome it as a friend. Gradually, become aware of yourself being held in the embrace of a devoted Presence. Be as an infant in a cradle, slowly swayed back and forth in the silence. There is no need to do anything except let yourself be peacefully rocked by this One who knows and loves you as you are.

For Reflection/Journaling

1. Write a prayer to the one whom you perceive to be the divine Presence. If you sense a great gap or a hard barrier between you and the divine Presence, write about that.

2. Have this Presence write a message to you about your current situation.
3. Record on a small notepaper what you sense needs to be "let go." If you do not know, simply place question marks. Hold the paper in your open hands. Sit quietly. When you feel ready, take the paper, tear it up, and discard it as a sign of your willingness to let go of whatever is required.

CHAPTER FIVE

The Morning Will Come

*I will keep still and wait like the night
with starry vigil and its head bent low
with patience.... The morning will surely
come, the darkness will vanish....*[18]

—Rabindranath Tagore

A clear night filled with the radiance of a zillion stars looks radically different from a cloudy sky darkened with the rumblings of an approaching storm. Our inner world portrays similar scenes. It mirrors the turbulent sky of the external world—those days, months (years, perhaps) of darkness that overwhelm our inner domain with turmoil and emptiness. The radiant, star-filled sky, on the other hand, compares internally to the treasurable experiences of someone, or something, shining hope into our inner sphere. Just as the dark of the cosmos reveals the vast array of stars, so our spirit's night gifts us with a sensitivity to experiences of light that help us find strength and courage to go on.

The stars, those beautiful lights of the universe, continually reach me with hope and comfort. When I walk under their visible presence, I feel wrapped in the womb of night, nurtured, tended to, and loved. I often yearn to walk in the dark of night but am usually too fearful to do so by myself. However, in the summer that I celebrated my fiftieth birthday, I decided to camp alone in the Sangre de Cristo Mountains. I knew I'd have some fear, but I also knew I wanted to ritualize that significant transition of aging.

I'll never forget being awakened that night by a brilliant light casting the tree branches' dark shadows on my tent. At first I thought morning had come in the forest, but when I looked out my tent's window, I was absolutely astounded to see a full moon penetrating the darkness of the mountain. I arose without the slightest hesitation and walked out into the night of which I had been afraid. To my surprise, I felt not an iota of fear. Instead, I sensed a blessed presence drawing me into kinship with the creatures of the mountain and of all humanity. I stood and stood in the moonlight with that overwhelming, kind radiance surrounding my being. The night was still night. The darkness was still there—but the moonlight erased my resistance to it.

C. G. Jung wrote that from the soul's "primordial beginnings there has been a desire for light and an irrepressible urge to rise out of the primal darkness."[19] Accepting our current condition of interior cloudiness while also longing for the sky to clear constitutes an immense paradox for our soul's journey. A part of us will always yearn for seeing lucidly when we are in the valley of shadows. This is our gift of hope. We go on believing—especially when deep in the tomb of darkness—that a harbor light within us waits to be ignited.

In *Sacred Poems and Prayers of Love*, Mary Ford-Grabowsky quotes the wisdom of a Jewish mystic: "A person is like a bed of coals." Ford-Grabowsky then goes on to assure her readers, "The flame may burn low, detaching us from the beautiful beings of the world, but as long as a single spark is left, the fire can be kindled once more."[20]

This is, perhaps, what the mother of poet William Stafford meant when she always kept a candle lit in the corner of one room because she believed "a soul will drink a candle flame."[21] We cannot drink a candle flame when darkness swirls around and through us, but we, too, can keep an inner candle aglow in our dark domain, a glowing assurance that promises hope of better times. We do this by turning repeatedly in daily faith to the One Flame whose light never goes out in a corner of our soul.

I never cease to be amazed at the countless and surprising ways the light gradually comes and takes over the darkness. Even the smallest glimmer calls with a strong and vibrant message of encouragement. Have you ever noticed how a tiny candle breaks the blackness of a darkened room? The same holds true for those little pieces of light illuminating the dark rooms of our hearts. Spiritual teacher and author Gary Zukov believes that "a soul with no light will always come to know Light because there is so much assistance provided to each soul at all times."[22] Zukov refers to the light coming to us from inner and outer guides and teachers who show up unexpectedly and help direct us toward wisdom.

A brilliant radiance resides in us—the Divine Illumination of our souls. This radiance carries an immense energy of love and wisdom. Each of us bears this light everyday of our lives, even when the darkness looms so large that we feel sure the light will be extinguished. No wonder the hope-filled Jesus referred to himself as "the Light," spoke of us having light within us, and encouraged us to share this light with others (John 8:12; Matt 5:14–66).

Light encompasses a variety of meanings, depending on people's beliefs and experiences. I've come to understand light as a combination of the divine presence within my being, the spark of my soul, the aura of energy I have within and around me, and the luminous energy connecting every part of the universe. This inner light bears a resemblance to sunlight. The sun acts as a stimulus for growth. It sends forth warmth for the earth, ripens fruits and vegetables, and gives greater clarity to the beauty of a landscape. So, too, the many-faceted light of my being brings growth of spirit, clarity of mind, and ripened teachings.

A good friend, Dorothy, now deceased, lived with blindness for over thirty years. When I visited her, I never thought of Dorothy's blindness because so much light radiated from her presence. She once said to me, "I think we are all little pieces of light for one another." That comment led me to reach far into my memory. I quickly recalled people who were there exactly when I needed them. Their "sparks" of compassion, understanding, nonjudgment, and insight gifted me with hope during my starless nights. I know this to be true for others, as well. Often, I hear comments from retreatants who acknowledge they could never have made it through their tough times had it not been for those who stood by faithfully, kept on believing in them, and offered constant care and support.

The memory of another's light sustains us. I was aware of this when I joined in a Roman Catholic Mass on the Feast of All Saints. This took place within a small church in a poorer part of the city. Mostly children from a nearby inner-city elementary school participated in the liturgy. The celebrant asked those present to recall loved ones who had died during the past year and to think of these persons on the other side of life as now being filled with light, illuminated with the goodness of saints.

He then invited the children who had experienced a loved one's death during the past year to come forward and receive a lit candle in honor of the deceased person. As several dozen children walked forward, I was surprised by the number of children that death had touched. Each child received the light, carried it to the altar, and named the one that the light honored: "my brother, my sister, my dad, my grandmother…"

Tears filled my eyes as the flames of more and more candles shone on the altar. As I looked at them, I felt the presence of the ancestors, "the wise ones," the souls who have a "knowing" we've yet to perceive. The strength of their presence and the power of their goodness radiated from the altar to my heart. I thought, "If only these ancestors could speak to us, how much they could tell us about life's difficulties. Surely they would encourage us to trust in the Light within us."

Not long after that light-filled liturgy, the evening news carried a story about one person's light making a significant difference. When the fighting became fierce in Bosnia-Herzegovina, a general from France stood his ground and insisted the besieged victims be evacuated. He allowed not just the sick and wounded to be moved but also their relatives. Nearly seven hundred found safety because of his bold deed. When the media interviewed the general about his decision, he spoke of the pain and suffering he witnessed. I noticed his eyes—they held a deep and luminous compassion. This inner light obviously gave him the courage to reach out to those in the depths of despair. One person's "little piece of light" penetrated the darkness of war and brought freedom and hope to hundreds of people.

I've experienced some of the strongest light coming from those who have suffered greatly. As the darkness breaks their hearts open, they become ever more vulnerable and compassionate. When this happens, walls of resistance, mental defenses and tightly held securities, fall away. Radiant kindness easily spreads because it has more room to shine.

Stephen Mitchell acknowledges, "Before we can share the light, we have to find it. When we embody it, we can't help sharing it, because it has no limits."[23] Our encounters with darkness push and press upon us until something within gives way. In these encounters, we "find" our light. This radiance naturally flows outward because we stop struggling and putting up barriers, or because the darkness gradually loses its strength, allowing the light to take over and flow outward.

A direct encounter with a person whose light illuminates another's darkness, or a simple gesture of kindheartedness—such as an understanding comment, a welcoming smile, a tender hug, or a compassionate message thoughtfully sent—blesses us with hope. Darkness lessens. Light surfaces. The author of *The Power of One* expresses it this way:

> Sometimes the slightest things clearly change
> the direction of our lives, the merest breath of
> circumstance, a random moment that connects

like a meteorite striking the earth. Lives have survived and changed direction on the strength of a chance remark.[24]

I recall a minister who endured long bouts of depression because of a seeming lack of success in his ministry. One day, he went to visit an ill parishioner. As he started to leave the room, the woman spoke to him, "You have been such an important person in my life. I want you to know that I have great love for you." These affirming words sailed straight into the minister's depression. He told me he couldn't believe it, but by the time he reached his office, he had already sensed that something had started changing direction inside of him. During the next several weeks, the depression lifted and he rejoiced in his welcomed rejuvenation.

The quickness with which the minister's darkness departed is quite unusual. Normally, the dissipation of internal darkness acts much like the dawning of a new day. The sun rarely comes bursting up from the horizon. Usually a first hint of light appears, then the changing coloration of the clouds, and finally the fullness of sunshine upon the land.

Something in us demands that light dissipate the darkness instantly. Not long ago, a friend of mine spoke to me about his process of being in therapy. He mused, "I wonder if I'm trying to hurry the process. I think I'm not being patient enough. It's hard not to be healthy immediately." How accurate his insight, and how essential that we maintain patience as we await the exodus of our interior nighttime.

It is not unusual for those who have been in deep depression or sorrow for a prolonged period to doubt the light's arrival when the first rays begin to lift onto the inner horizon. When light approaches, so do hesitation, doubt, confusion, and questions about the light's authenticity. Painful emotions associated with extended despondency have hung on for so long. How could it be that an end has arrived? The pessimistic, weary, beaten down, doubtful part of the self tends to respond to the glimpsed light with "Oh, this won't last…I can't afford to believe I might be feeling good again. I don't want to be disappointed…I must be imagining this…Is this really a turning point? Can I be happy again? I've forgotten how that feels. Can I trust it?"

I've watched this kind of hesitancy as newly hatched butterflies are released from a birthing box and given their freedom. They don't immediately fly away. Often the butterflies will sit for quite a while before they stretch their colored wings and lift off toward a flower or twig. Sometimes they wait to be strong enough—the blood of their body may need to be more fully circulated in their wings—and sometimes the wings are not quite dry enough. At times it appears as though the butterflies simply do not realize they are actually free to go whenever and wherever they choose.

One of my favorite stories about not seeing the "light" we yearn for came from a woman working in a country where numerous rainbows arched across the sky every day. She often expressed the wish that she could go stand in a rainbow. One day as she and her companions traveled, they noticed a magnificent rainbow a mile or so in front of them. She urged the driver to hurry toward it. When they arrived at the rainbow, the woman jumped out of the car and rushed over to it. To her surprise, she couldn't tell when she was in the rainbow. She kept calling to the others, "Am

I in it yet? Am I in it now?" "Yes, yes," they called back, "you're in it right now. You just can't see it, but we can."

Like standing in a rainbow, the light might encompass us but something about our inner terrain or our long bout with darkness keeps us from being able to see or accept it. We simply have to trust it is so. If we have others to assure us we are "standing in the light" when we find ourselves hesitant or disbelieving, we are fortunate, indeed.

This tentativeness or lack of belief that the light is actually present reminds me of one of the Easter stories. Before dawn, Mary of Magdala goes to the tomb to anoint the dead body of Jesus. She arrives and stands before the tomb. As her eyes adjust to the last shades of night, Mary is startled to see the tomb opened and the body missing. She expected to find death present in the darkness. She becomes confused. Where is the body? The doubtful or not-yet-wise part of herself concludes that someone must have removed or stolen it. She does not yet comprehend that Jesus has been raised from the dead. Because she is focused on the death of her Beloved, Mary cannot perceive that the light has overcome this darkness.

Mary departs and runs to tell others that the body of Jesus has been taken away. Later, when dawn lights up the land, Mary returns to the tomb. She gathers up courage and through her tears, she peers into the emptiness. This time she sees two white-robed messengers of light. She tells them of her sorrow and then turns to leave the hollow space where death once laid. As Mary turns toward the light, she notices the risen Jesus in the garden but still does not comprehend the ending of death, mistaking him for the gardener. Because she is overwhelmed with sorrow, this radical transformation of new life remains incomprehensible to Mary. Only when Jesus speaks her name does the truth of resurrection finally penetrate Mary's awareness. The sound of her name breaks open her wall of disbelief. Mary's consciousness awakens to the resurrected Light, and she finally moves beyond the darkness (cf. John 20:1–18).

Time and again, life calls us to peer into the entombed parts of ourselves, to look into our experiences of darkness, however large or small, and to review what has "risen." Perhaps we are as startled as Mary of Magdala to find that the "dead body" of our grief, our troubles, our depression, no longer resides there. Gratitude eventually arises as we recognize how we have moved out of the once-prevalent darkness. We acknowledge what we have learned, how we have changed, and the qualities of spirit that now radiate more fully from us.

As we turn away from darkness, we see the light of our restored life in evidence through our widening compassion, our reassured sense of self, and our evolving appreciation of simple joys and the gift of being alive. Like an owl weaving through the black night seeking food, we realize we did find nourishment even when we felt most depleted and seemingly forsaken.

We rarely step beyond our entombed times without carrying some wisdom with us. Often this perception includes knowing more clearly how life consists of, and needs, both light and darkness. We understand the truth of what the renowned Vietnamese Buddhist teacher, Thich Nhat Hanh, came to understand out of his prolonged exile:

> According to the creation story in the biblical book of Genesis, God said, "Let there be light." I

like to imagine that light replied, saying, "God, I have to wait for my twin brother, darkness, to be with me. I can't be there without the darkness." God asked, "Why do you need to wait? Darkness is there." Light answered, "In that case, I am also already there."

If we focus exclusively on pursuing happiness, we may regard suffering as something to be ignored or resisted. We think of it as something that gets in the way of happiness. But the art of happiness is also the art of knowing how to suffer well. If we know how to use our suffering, we can transform it and suffer much less. Knowing how to suffer well is essential to true happiness.[25]

This might be the most significant message we carry with us from the tomb: Where darkness dwells, light also abides. The sage of scripture trusted this truth long ago when he wrote in Psalm 139:

I will say, "Let the darkness cover me,
and the night wrap itself around me,"
even darkness to you is not dark,
and night is as clear as the day. (vv. 11–12)

Prayer

O God,
as I look back at my life
I see many little pieces of light.

They have given me hope and comfort
in my bleak and weary times.
I thank you for the radiance
of a dark sky full of stars,
and for the faithful light of dawn
that follows every turn of darkness.
I thank you for loved ones and strangers
whose inner beacons of light
warmed and welcomed my pain.
I thank you for your presence in my depths,
protecting, guiding, reassuring, loving.
I thank you for all those life-surprises
that sparked a bit of hope in my ashes.
And, yes, I thank you for my darkness,
(the unwanted companion I shun and avoid)
because this pushy intruder comes with truth
and reveals my hidden treasures.

~Joyce Rupp

Meditation

Call to mind a deceased person whom you admire, someone who is a "mentor of hope" for you. What qualities of that person are of most help to you now? Picture that person being with you at your favorite place in nature or elsewhere. Imagine the two of you sitting peacefully together. The longer you remain with one another, the more you sense that person's qualities growing stronger in you. Continue to be present to each other for as long as you wish. When it is time to say farewell, express your gratitude for whatever you have received. Take a deep breath and let yourself rest in what you have just experienced, knowing you can invite this beloved being into your life whenever you wish.

For Reflection/Journaling

1. What would you want to say to the person who is a "mentor of hope" for you?
2. Recall times in your life when you moved through a tough period and recovered a sense of well-being. Describe one of these times. How did you eventually move beyond the struggle?
3. Light a candle and hold it between your hands. Notice the light and warmth coming forth from the candle. Extend the candle in front of you as a symbol of your hope for the future, then set the candle down and write about the guiding, healing Light within you.

Epilogue

In his novel *The Heart of the Hunter*, Laurens van der Post describes a poignant scene in the midst of the Kalahari desert. He camps there with local bushmen, and they sit around a circle of fire. The absence of any artificial light allows for a world of complete darkness once one moves beyond the campfire. The stars hang low in the sky, their brilliance not only seen but heard. Van der Post describes the sound of the stars as "this intense electric murmur at one's ears." Then he sees the outline of a bush woman holding her young infant up to the stars. She is singing some kind of chant with her face lifted to the sky.

When van der Post asks the local bushmen what the woman is doing, they tell him she is asking the stars to take the heart of her child and give him "something of the heart of a star in return...because the stars have heart in plenty." The heart of the stars is a hunting heart, one that seeks with courage and finds the inner nourishment needed for life.[26] When I read this explanation, I thought of all of us who have been in darkness. When the light comes back, it is as though we have a "child" within us coming to birth.

This "child" may be a new way of living or loving, a deepened sense of self-esteem, a turning over of our old ways, a ripening of our past ideas and beliefs, a wisdom rising from our grieving, or any other new and fresh development. If only we could, as the bush woman did with her child, take this part of us and hold it tenderly, trustingly, in our open hands. We could lovingly hold up whatever waits to be born in us, asking that this newness be blessed with the heart of the stars. We could pray that we receive a "hunting heart," so that we might seek with courage and live with confidence, believing that what we need for our soul will be given.

We carry our greatest treasure within us: a piece of light that will forever shine, a radiance always lighting our way home. Let us trust this light. It will never go out.

Notes

1. Thomas Moore, *Care of the Soul* (New York: HarperCollins, l992), 21.

2. Joan Halifax, *The Fruitful Darkness* (San Francisco: HarperSanFrancisco, 1993), 179.

3. Sue Monk Kidd, *When the Heart Waits* (San Francisco: Harper and Row, 1990), 152.

4. Bryce Courtenay, *The Power of One* (New York: Ballantine Books, 1991), 47.

5. Carol Pregent, *When a Child Dies* (Notre Dame: Ave Maria Press, 1992), 59.

6. Stephen Levine, *Healing into Life and Death* (New York: Doubleday Anchor Books, 1987), 222.

7. Robbi Sommers, "My Fight for Justice," *Reader's Digest*, April 1993.

8. Taken from the *New Revised Standard Version: Catholic Edition* of the Bible, Copyright © 1989 and 1993, by the Division of Christian Education of the National Council of the Churches of Christ in the United States of America. Used by permission. All rights reserved.

9. Rabindranath Tagore, *Gitanjali*, no. 99 (New York: Macmillan, 1913), 111.

10. Nor Hall, *The Moon and the Virgin* (San Francisco: Harper and Row, 1980), 223.

11. William Bridges, *Transitions* (Reading, MA: Addison Wesley, 1980), 117.

12. Maureen Murdock, *The Heroine's Journey* (Boston: Shambhala, 1990), 88.

13. Macrina Wiederkehr, *A Tree Full of Angels* (San Francisco: Harper and Row, 1988), 46.

14. Ann Keiffer, *Gift of the Dark Angel* (San Diego: LuraMedia, 1991), 114.

15. Thomas Merton, *New Seeds of Contemplation* (New York: New Directions, 2007), 221.

16. Kidd, *When the Heart Waits*, 146.

17. Colleen Fulmer, "Rock Me Gentle," from *Her Wings Unfurled*, Loretto Spirituality Network, Albany, CA, cassette tape, 1989, https://www.youtube.com/user/ColleenFulmer.

18. Tagore, *Gitanjali*, no. 19, 37.

19. C. G. Jung, *Memories, Dreams, Reflections* (New York: Random House, 1961), 269.

20. Mary Ford-Grabowsky, *Sacred Poems and Prayers of Love* (New York: Doubleday, 1998), 4–5.

21. William Stafford, "Lighting a Candle," in *A Scripture of Leaves* (Elgin, IL: Brethren Press, 1989), 50.

22. Gary Zukov, *The Seat of the Soul* (New York: Simon & Schuster, 1989), 71.

23. Stephen Mitchell, *The Gospel According to Jesus* (New York: HarperCollins, 1991), 161.

24. Courtenay, *The Power of One*, 62.

25. Thich Nhat Hanh, "Five Practices for Nurturing Happiness," *Shambhala Sun*, March 2015, 40–45.

26. Laurens van der Post, *The Heart of the Hunter* (New York: Wm. Morrow, 1961), 32–33.

Study Guide

Chapter 1: The Land of Darkness

1. How would you describe your understanding of "the land of darkness?"
2. What is the most difficult for you when something you value is taken from you?
3. Have you, or has someone you know, experienced some aspect of darkness, such as depression or the "dark night of the soul?"
4. The author quotes Joan Halifax on "befriending our darkness." Do you agree or disagree with this approach? What are some ways one might "befriend the darkness?"
5. Are there other questions you would add to those the author raises on page 12?

Chapter 2: Leave the Hall Light On

1. Describe your experience of fear. What has helped you to meet the fears in your life?
2. The author writes, "The emotions associated with darkness are ones we often experience in

times of grief." With which emotions of grief do you most resonate? From your experience, are there other non-grief emotions associated with darkness?

3. With which of the stories of fear that the author relates do you most identify, and why?
4. Name some of your "hall lights."
5. Is there anything you would add to this chapter that could help someone in darkness to cope with his or her fears?

Chapter 3: Silent Stirrings in the Tomb

1. What thoughts, feelings, and memories does the word *tomb* evoke in you?
2. Does the suggestion of ritualizing Holy Saturday seem of value? If so, how might you go about ritualizing the "in-between" of Calvary and Easter?
3. Recall a past experience when you were "in the tomb." How did "resurrection" occur?
4. What is your response to the author's comment regarding the "false voice" in some resources and therapeutic curatives?
5. What Bible story most speaks to you about the movement out of darkness and into the light?

Chapter 4: Separate Bedrooms

1. Have you, or has someone you know, felt a great distance in your/their relationship with the Divine?

2. If you were to give a summary of this chapter in a few sentences, what would you say?
3. How has your understanding and experience of divinity changed? What led to that change?
4. The author writes, "There are numerous ways in which the darkest moments of our spiritual lives teach us and guide us." Of the ways suggested, which ones concur with your lived experience?
5. What is your response to such words as *surrender*, *yield*, and *let go*? Are there other words you prefer to use when referring to the process of consenting to what transformation requires?

Chapter 5: The Morning Will Come

1. If asked about the light in your soul, how would you respond?
2. As you look back on your experience of darkness, what "little pieces of light" have been especially significant?
3. Describe how you have grown or changed due to a dark time.
4. When you peer into the tomb of your life, what do you see?
5. As you reflect on the content and approach of this book, is there anything missing that you want to add? What did you find of most value?